Dear Nature Lover

Without question trees take first place among our landscape plants. Not only are they the largest but also the most impressive of all our flora. Since time immemorial they have been shrouded in mystery for human beings, possessing magical powers, inhabited by good and bad spirits that may bring good luck or bad.

In the new *Barron's Coniferous Trees* you will find the most commonly cultivated European conifers, those either native to Europe or that have been transplanted over the course of time from the temperate zones of North America and Asia. These conifers are also cultivated in America. Many are native species, while others are found in gardens and parks. One hundred and twenty photographs, taken specifically for this book, and clearly written text describe the general appearance of the trees and focus on such important details as branches, needles, trunk, and bark.

The species shown here grow in fields and forests and also in parks and gardens where one may encounter the numerous cultivars, which often differ greatly—not only in the external form but also in the color of the needles—from the species type displaying the characteristic species hallmarks. *Barron's Coniferous Trees* limits itself to the species-specific type, which the layperson must first be able to identify in order to recognize the hybrid varieties.

Besides its specific function in helping with identification, this pocket tree guide provides additional interesting information about the special characteristics of conifers that is not to be found in any other tree identification book. The more we know about the nature surrounding us, the more we can understand and love it.

The new *Barron's Coniferous Trees* fits into one's pocket. It has a sturdy cover, is lightweight, and is therefore the ideal companion for nature walks.

S0-BZW-825

Photograph on front cover: Cedar of Lebanon; back cover: Mountain forest.

Silver Fir

(top) The needles grow opposite each other (parted) on the twig; they are glossy on top and have two white lines. (center) The upright cones are green at first, later brown; they do not drop. (bottom) The sap spots are clearly recognizable on the light, smooth bark of young trees.

The silver fir is found in the mountains of western, central, and southern Europe, where it is usually encountered at altitudes of 6562 ft (2000 m). It can live to be 500 years old. The scientific species name *alba* means "white," but it is not entirely clear whether this refers to the color of the white underside of the needles or to the grayish-white bark. The wood of the silver fir is easy to work and is used, among other things, for sounding boards of musical instruments. There are also some ornamental forms of the silver fir.

Scientific Name: *Abies alba*
Family: Pine
Form: Up to 164 ft (50 m) tall, slender, cone-shaped, with horizontally projecting branches; with age the crown forms the typical "stork's nest."
Twigs: Gray-brown, coarsely hairy, not fissured.
Needles: ½–1 in (15–30 mm) long; flat; upper side glossy dark green; underside has two white lines; notched at the tip; usually parted in double rows. The needle cover varies widely according to location and amount of light received.
Cones: 4–6 in (10–16 cm) long; erect, as with all fir species; do not drop.
Bark: Gray-white in juvenile trees; glossy with sap ducts; in adult ones cracked and rough.

Similar Species: The giant or lowland fir (*Abies grandis*) grows almost 328 ft (100 m) high in its native habitat on the West Coast of North America. In Europe, where it has been growing since the first half of the 19th century, it is not much larger than the silver fir. Because it grows quickly, it is planted in parks and forests. Differentiating the giant fir from the silver fir is not easy. The giant fir can be recognized by its bark—brownish-red at first, later dark-brown—and the longer needles, up to 2½ in (60 mm) long, which are also parted in double rows, although the upper row consists of shorter needles. There are many cultivars of this species.

Nordmann's Fir

In growth habit the Nordmann's fir resembles the silver fir, cone-shaped at first, becoming narrow and columnar in shape with age. The tree comes from Asia Minor and the western Caucasus, where at altitudes of 3280 ft (1000 m) to 6562 ft (2000 m) it forms dense forests and becomes approximately 230 ft (70 m) tall. The Nordmann's fir was brought to Europe around the middle of the 19th century. Originally it was planted in parks in place of the native silver fir because of its better growth habit and thicker needle cover. Since then it has also been cultivated as a forest tree and appears more and more frequently on the market as a Christmas tree. The tree requires high humidity and tolerates city air poorly. There are some ornamental forms, such as a "Glauca" (a bluish one), as well as a dwarf and a weeping form.

(top) The stubby needles are situated around the twig. This shows the glossy upper side of the needle. (center) The male flowers look like tiny cones; they grow at the ends of the twigs. The juvenile cones stand erect, as do those of all firs. (bottom) Trunk with branches.

Scientific Name: *Abies nordmanniana*
Family: Pine
Form: Up to 90 ft (30 m) tall, with branches down to the ground, even when old, especially if the tree is freestanding. Branches dense, in whorls, somewhat upturned.
Twigs: At first smooth and glossy, olive-yellow; later pinkish-brown, usually hairy.

Needles: ¾ in–1½ in (20–35 mm) long; longitudinal dent; blunt at the end or notched; leatherlike; top side glossy green, underside with two white lines; situated around the twig, less dense on the underside than on the upper side; forward-pointing, toward the end of the branch.

Cones: 4½–6 in (12–15 cm) long and 2 in (5 cm) thick; erect; confined to the tip area, often very numerous; they are brown and resinous; the covering scales curve outward and have a protruding "hook."

Bark: In young trees dull, light gray, and smooth; later dark gray and peeling in thick flakes.

Note: Can best be differentiated from the silver fir by the needles. These are shorter, thicker, and slightly parted.

(top) Branch ends seen from above and below; underneath the needles are spread flat and have two narrow white lines. (center) The cones are remarkably large up to 9¾ in [25 cm] long and grow even on relatively young trees. (bottom) The trunk is at first smooth and has sap spots.

One of the most beautiful firs when it is able to develop free-standing. It originates in western North America (Oregon, Washington) where it grows to 262 ft (80 m) tall in the mountains. In Europe, where it was introduced in 1930, it reaches only a height of 66–98 ft (20–30 m). The noble fir's growth is narrowly conical and in the United States is most often found in parklands. The Latin name *procera* means "long, tall, slender." Besides the common variety, the bluish form, "Glauca," is frequently planted.

Scientific Name: *Abies procera*
Family: Pine
Form: In open space the trunk is furnished densely with branches all the way to the ground; lower branches point markedly downward; in young trees the crown is conical, later spreading to columnar shape.
Twigs: Brownish-red, not fissured, very hairy.
Needles: Soft; 10–14 in (25–35 cm) long; slightly grooved, rounded at the tip; blue-green on the upper side, underside with two narrow, dull white lines; the needles grow very thickly; on the underside of the twig they are spread out flat on both sides of the twig (parted); the row of needles on the upper side is shorter, points

forward, and is depressed toward the twig.

Cones: Cylindrical; very large 6–10 in (15–25 cm) long, 2¾–3 in (7–8 cm) thick; green at first, later purplish-brown with pale green outer scales.

Bark: Smooth, silvery gray with many crosswise sap ducts; in age dark brown and deeply fissured. (The sap ducts secrete thinly flowing resin—as is true of other conifers.)

Similar Species: Red fir (*Abies magnifica*) originates in California and was introduced to Europe around 1850. In its native habitat it grows 196–262 ft (60–80 m) tall; in Europe probably barely half that height. The red fir has a sturdy trunk, grows narrowly conical, and is very evenly shaped. In contrast to the noble fir there are no sap spots on the young trunk. Furthermore, the needles are longer (up to 1½ in [40 mm]), stiff, and not parted.

White Fir

(top) The soft needles are the same color on both sides (hence the scientific name *concolor*); the crescent-shaped upward bend of the needles is typical; this positively identifies the tree. In shade the twigs have fewer needles, which grow in only two rows. (bottom) In the open, the tree has branches all the way to the ground; with age the lower trunk is bare; the bark is longitudinally fissured.

A very decorative tree that, especially in the open, with its gray-green needled foliage reaching to the ground, is the ornament of any garden or park. The white fir is one conifer that can be identified even by the nonexpert without difficulty and recognized because of its extraordinarily long needles, which are curved upward in a sickle shape. The tree's habitat is Southern California, Utah, and Colorado to Mexico; it was imported to Europe at the end of the 19th century. The scientific name (*concolor*) refers to the color of the needles, which is the same on both sides. In Europe the tree is usually planted in parks and gardens, rarely in forests. The white fir tolerates dry ground and city air and is therefore among the trees with a future in thickly settled areas. There are some cultivars that differ in the color and the length and width of the needles—however, the needles are always bent.

Scientific Name: *Abies concolor*
Family: Pine
Form: Loosely pyramidal; height up to 131 ft (40 m) tall; the branches project horizontally; freestanding trees have branches to the bottom of the trunk.

Twigs: Gray-green when young; gray-brown and bare when old.

Needles: Both sides dull gray-green to gray-blue; thick; leathery soft; green center trough on the underside; 1½–3 in (40–80 mm) long and bending upward in a sickle shape; in shade only two rows, in sunlight denser.

Cones: Clustered at top of tree; some 4 in (10 cm) long; blue-green at first, later dark violet; the cones stay on the tree and do not drop.

Bark: Gray, rough, with many sap marks.

Douglas Fir

The Douglas fir is neither a fir nor a spruce and has its own genus. However, it does have qualities in common with both of them: It looks like a broad-spreading fir and, like them, it drops its cones to the ground. On the other hand, its needles have the characteristics of the spruce, for they sit directly on the twig and when they fall or are torn away, they leave only a round scar rather than a bump as with the fir. The scientific name *Pseudotsuga* indicates certain similarities to the *Tsuga* (hemlock spruce): soft needles, which on young twigs are often parted in double rows. The Douglas fir was at home in Europe before the Ice Age but then died out. It survived in North America, especially in the Northwest, from Canada to the southern Rockies. In the 18th century it was again introduced to Europe by the Scottish horticulturalist and botanist David Douglas. Since that time the tree has become an important forest tree but it has also been planted in parks and gardens. The Douglas fir can live for as long as 600 years; it is fast-growing and produces valuable wood.

(top) When one runs one's hand over the needles, one notices how soft they are: on the undersides they have two whitish lines. (center) Douglas fir cones hang down and later fall to the ground; the protruding scale leaves are typical. (bottom) The bark of the older tree is dark and fissured.

Scientific Name:
Pseudotsuga menziesii
Family: Pine
Form: In Europe, up to 131 ft

(40 m) tall. In America, up to 328 ft (100 m), broad and conical. In young trees the limbs point upward; later they are horizontal, with hanging branches; limbs grow down the trunk to the ground when the tree is freestanding.

Twigs: Somewhat hairy; at first bright yellow, then reddish-brown, later gray-brown.

Needles: ¾–1in (20–30 mm) long; soft; flat; end blunt to pointed; yellow-green to blue-green, undersides with two whitish lines; on young twigs two rows, parted, but otherwise situated all around the twig; strong scent when rubbed.

Cones: 2–4 in (5–10 cm) long; cone scales broad, smooth, with rounded edges; outer scales with longer, narrow, triangular tongues.

Bark: Gray-green when young, many resin ducts; later dark and fissured.

Hemlock

A very decorative conifer with irregular habit and slightly pendent limbs and branches. It originates in eastern North America and grows there in cool and often rocky places, especially in damp ravines. Often called the hemlock spruce, the hemlock has a genus of its own. It was brought to Europe around 1740 and has become widely distributed since then. It is found mostly in parks and gardens; forest cultivation is undertaken only occasionally because of the mediocre quality of the wood. The hemlock prefers damp, not too hot locations and also thrives in semishade. The tree is called hemlock after the poisonous plant of that name whose scent the rubbed needles are said to have. However, *Tsuga* is not poisonous!

Scientific Name: *Tsuga canadensis*
Family: Pine
Form: Up to 98 ft (30 m) high, irregular, broadly conical. In its native American habitat it has a single trunk; in Europe often several; branches horizontal or steeply upslanting, irregularly placed.
Twigs: Bright brown, hairy.
Needles: Only ⅕–½ inch (5–15 mm) long; soft; flat, blunt, not crenated, palpably rough-edged, gradually tapering from base to point; upper

(top) The needles are very short and stubby, taper from base to tip, are parted, and have two white lines on the underside. The cones are only 1 in (2.5 cm) long. (center) Reddish-purple male flowers shortly before pollination. (bottom) The branches extend horizontally from the trunk.

side glossy dark green, underside with two white lines; parted on twigs.

Cones: Up to 1 in (2.5 cm) long; oval; on a short stem; scales rounded.

Bark: Gray-brown, light, fissured.

Similar Species: The western hemlock (*Tsuga heterophylla* Sarg.) comes from western North America, was brought to Europe in the middle of the 19th century, where it grows in parks and gardens.

Heterophylla means "different-leaved," which is seen in the various leaf lengths along the twig; this, however, is also the case with *T. canadensis*. The most important difference is in the needles—in the western hemlock they do not taper but remain the same size from the base to the tip—and in the cones, which do not have a stem.

Norway Spruce

(top) Branch with lateral twig on which the sharply pointed needles grow all around; they may be somewhat bent. (center) Red female flowers from which later a (hanging) cone develops. (bottom) In contrast to the light trunk of the silver fir, the trunk of the spruce is reddish-violet.

The spruce is the most important forest tree in central Europe today. Its native habitats are the European mountains of the middle and northern regions; thus they can thrive even at elevations of 6562 ft (2000 m). Scarcely any other tree has so many growth forms, some arising naturally but some also through hybridizing—a circumstance that makes it difficult for the layperson to recognize the Norway spruce and differentiate it from the other spruce varieties. However, a good identifying characteristic of spruces is that they drop their cones and do not retain them on the trees as the firs do. (There are two further distinctions: Spruce needles arise from small bumps, which stay on the branches even if the needles fall off; in the fir the needles grow *directly* from the branch and leave behind only a tiny scar. Furthermore, in the spruce the cones *hang*; in the fir they are *erect* on the branch.) The Norway spruce may live to be 500 years old; its wood is usable for many different purposes. The genus name *Picea* derives from the Latin word *pix*, which means "pitch" and reminds us that at one time pitch was obtained from the resin of the spruce and other conifers.

Scientific Name: *Picea abies*

Family: Pine
Form: Up to 164 ft (50 m) tall, pointed-conical. Branches situated in whorls, the upper ones aimed upward, the lower ones pointing downward but toward the end of the branch pointing upward again.
Twigs: Reddish-yellow; bare or hairy.
Needles: Less than ½ to nearly 1 in (10–25 mm) long; straight or curved; square in cross-section, pointed; somewhat prickly; dark green on all sides; radially positioned on upright twigs, on horizontal ones parted underneath.
Cones: 4–6 in (10–15 cm) long; at first green or reddish, later light brown. The scales firmly fixed; at the edge tapering to a more or less pronounced tongue.
Bark: Reddish, with thin scales.

Oriental Spruce

A stately evergreen whose branches reach down to the ground when it stands in the open; at a distance cannot be distinguished from other spruces without closer examination. Seen close up, it is easily recognized by its very short, blunt needles (most spruce species have sharp needles). Its habitat is the Caucasus and Taurus mountains; there it constitutes large forests at elevations of 6562 ft (2000 m). Although it was discovered in the 18th century, *Picea orientalis* was first brought to Europe in 1840 and proliferated there. It is found in parks and gardens, also often in trimmed hedges. It has no special requirements for soil and location and can even be planted in shade, since lack of sun does not cause it to drop its needles. There are also some cultivars (golden, dwarf, and weeping forms).

Scientific Name: *Picea orientalis*
Family: Pine
Form: Up to 98 ft (30 m) tall. In its native habitat up to 197 ft (60 m.); conical. Branches to ground, horizontal or up-tilting, ends slightly upward-pointing, in irregular whorls.
Twigs: Light brown or whitish; hairy.
Needles: Only ⅕–⅓ in (6–8 mm) long; square in cross sec-

(top) The needles of the *Picea orientalis* are only ⅕–⅓ in (6–8 mm) long, the shortest of all the spruces; they are rounded at the end and look lacquered. The twig has needles all around it. (center) Branches with male flowers. (bottom) Trunk with bark; on the young tree it breaks off in small, round flakes.

tion; thick and stiff, rounded at the end; dark green on all sides and looking lacquered, without white lines; on the upper side of the twig aiming forward so that the twig is covered; the needle cushions are very distinct.

Cones: 2–3½ in (6–9 cm), linear; at first green to purple-red, later brown; scales broad and round, with a smooth edge.

Bark: Brown with a few fissures, soon peels off in small scales.

This spruce is easily identifiable by its unusually small growth form. With its slender trunk and, when freestanding, branches hanging down to the ground, the Serbian spruce is one of the most decorative of the conifers. It is native to Serbia and Bosnia in southern Yugoslavia, where it grows on steep mountain slopes. At one time it grew across entire mountains up to elevations of 4921 ft (1500 m). Since then it has been severely diminished in its native habitat but has become widely distributed over the rest of Europe. It is the mostly commonly encountered spruce in parks, cemeteries, and gardens. Besides its ornamental function, it is popular for planting where there is not much space available. *Omorika* is the Serbian word for spruce.

Scientific Name: *Picea omorika*

Family: Pine

Form: Up to 98 ft (30 m) tall, very slim conical shape. Thickening where branches begin, with a hollow beneath it; branches extend horizontally, are aimed down and then up again in an arc shape.

Twigs: Brown, hairy.

Needles: 1/3–1/2 in (8–15 mm) long; square, but compressed flat, producing a keel above and below; sharply pointed (in

(top) In contrast to the Norway spruce, the needles of the Serbian spruce have two small white lines on the undersides and the needles are often curved. (center) Two ripe, hanging cones; they are a glossy cinnamon brown. (bottom) The trunk is scaly, and there is a swelling at the base of the branches.

young trees) or blunt with a small point (in older trees); shining dark green on top, with two white lines on underside; needles slightly bent; located around the twig but still occasionally somewhat parted on the underside; the upper needles often curved upward so that the white undersides are visible.

Cones: 1–2 in (3–6 cm) long, tapering; dark blue-black when young; glossy cinnamon brown when mature; stiff scales, broad, roundish, toothed along the edges; even young trees have numerous cones.

Bark: Orange-brown with papery scales, which later become square and hard.

Colorado Blue Spruce

(top) The needles of the Colorado blue spruce are stiff and sharp; the twig has needles all around it. The blue form "Glauca" is shown here. (center) The cones pictured have rounded scales, but they are often also seen with an elongated tongue. (bottom) The branches extend from the trunk horizontally.

The Colorado blue spruce is a common ornamental tree in European parks and gardens. The various blue-toned forms, which, as is usual with conifers are known under the general name "Glauca," enjoy great popularity. Other forms—green or blue—have dwarf growth habits or weeping branches. Sometimes the Colorado blue spruce is also planted in forests. It comes from southwestern North America (Rocky Mountains, Utah, Colorado) and grows there at elevations of 10,827 ft (3300 m) as a solitary tree. Around 1860 the tree was brought to Europe. It shows noteworthy insensitivity to the smoke and dust of cities and tolerance for various soils and locations.

Scientific Name: *Picea pungens*
Family: Pine
Form: Up to 98 ft (30 m) tall, conical shape, dense growth. Very fat at the bottom, branches extending horizontally, bending upward in older trees, dense, in regular whorls.
Twigs: Bare; at first smooth and light brown, later brown and then blackish.
Needles: ¾–1⅙ in (20–30 mm) long; square; stiff, coming to a needle-sharp point; distributed around the entire twig, often somewhat sparser on the underside of the twig; matt

green to silver-gray or blue-gray, same color on all four sides.

Cones: 2¾–4 in (7–10 cm) long; light brown, with very thin but still stiff cone scales with a tapering tongue at the front edge, which is notched at the end.

Bark: Young, gray-brown; old, darker, with long, deep fissures and peeling in small flakes.

Similar Species: *Asperata* (*Picea asperata*) with paper-thin bark scales, shorter needles ½–¾ in (10–18 mm) and reddish-brown cones whose leathery scales are entire and not elongated at the front edge. In addition there is the *Engelmannii* spruce (*Picea engelmanii*). It is also grown in forests as well as in parks and gardens (in Northern Europe). The square needles have white lines on all four surfaces.

Giant Sequoia/Giant Redwood

(top) The needles resemble the scale leaves of the cypress, are distributed spirally around the twig, and grow with the point canted outward. (center) A ripe cone with the typical broad-rhomboid-shaped, bulging scale. (bottom) The trunk has a soft bark and is wide at the bottom.

There are two "big trees"—the *Sequoiadendron giganteum* described here, which is also winter-hardy to some extent in central Europe, and the coastal sequoia *(Sequoia sempervirens)*, which thrives in warmer locations. While the former can grow to about 328 ft (100 m) in its habitat in the Sierra Nevada in California, the coastal sequoia, which also comes from California, can reach 361 ft (110 m). *Sequoiadendron giganteum* can live to be 3500 years old. It was discovered in 1850, and very soon afterward the seeds arrived in England. Since then the tree has been planted in parks in the rest of Europe, where it has already reached heights of 90 ft (30 m). Attempts to use it for forestation are also underway; however, it has turned out that the wood of European trees— unlike those in America—is very soft and hardly usable.

Scientific Name:
Sequoiadendron giganteum
Family: Taxodium
Form: Symmetrical, slender-conical, mostly with pointed crown, sometimes also with rounded one. Trunk with a very broad base up to some 6½ ft (2 m) from base, then narrower; the side limbs near the top reach upward; those under them are horizontal; those at

the bottom pendent but nevertheless bent upward at the end.

Twigs and Branchlets: Stiff, curved upward at the ends.

Needles: Distributed spirally along the whole twig; $^1/_{10}$–$^3/_{10}$ in (3–8 mm) long; blue-green; they are close-lying and thus resemble long, tapering leaf scales that turn out at the tips.

Cones: Egg-shaped; 2–3 in (5–8 cm) long; on long stems; the older cones lying under the tree are black-brown and only slightly opened; the scales are broad-rhomboid in shape, and bulging.

Bark: Red, extraordinarily thick bark; deep cracks; spongy, can be indented with the fingers.

Common Juniper

The juniper grows in sunny, dry places and is at home in most of the northern temperate zone. The numerous variations of its hybrid forms are often found in the garden. The juniper can live to be 800 years old. Its dense, tough, but yet soft wood is popular for wood working. Juniper berries are found in the kitchen as well as in the pharmacy; they are also used for such familiar alcoholic drinks as gin. Common juniper is dioecious.

(top) The stiff, piercingly sharp needles are situated in threes around the twig; a white line can be seen on the top side. The round fruits, the "berry cones," are greenish at first, blue-black when mature, and frosted bluish. (bottom) The trunk is often not visible; it peels in long strips.

Scientific Name: *Juniperus communis*
Family: Cypress
Form: Tree or bush, pillar-shaped, up to 26 ft (8 m) tall; trunk with branches all the way to the ground.
Needles: The common juniper has only needles, not like some other juniper species which have scale leaves. They occur in threes around the twig; stiff and sharply pointed; they do not run in a continuous row around the twig; up to ½ in (15 mm) long; somewhat canoe-shaped, gray-green, marked on the upper side with a wide, whitish line.
Cones: "Berry cones," spherical, plump, ⅓–⅖ in (7–9 mm) thick; greenish at first, then blue-black and bluish when ripe.
Bark: Gray- or red-brown,

with long fissures and peeling tatters of bark.

Similar Species: *Juniperus squamata Meyeri* is a cultivar of the species *J. squamata*, which comes from the mountains of central Asia and is frequently used in gardens. The blue-gray color is typical.

Needles: Also placed in threes around the twig, stiff and sharp, up to ⅓ in (7 mm) long; curved; upper side blue-green, underside blue-white.

Cones: Berry cones, red-brown at first, then black.

English Yew

The characteristic features of the common yew are the extraordinarily dark color of the needles and the fact that these trees grow very tall, even in shade, singly and in small groups, preferring alkaline soil. The yew is at home all across the northern hemisphere. In earlier days crossbows and bows were made from its hard, red-brown, very tough wood (the scientific name *Taxus* means "bow"). Today the wood is used for furniture (English furniture). The yew can live to be more than 2000 years old. In mythology it is the tree of death, and it is still planted in cemeteries as well as in parks. Since the Middle Ages it has been declining in Europe, so that today the tree is a protected species in many countries. In the United States it is a shrub commonly found in yards. Needles and seeds are very poisonous! There are numerous cultivars, which differ from the species type in color of needles or in growth form.

(top) The needles of the yew are flat and have a small point; they are situated in two rows (parted) along the twig. (center) This conifer does not produce cones but so-called "pseudo berries." The trunks of young yews are smooth; the outer bark peels off like paper.

Scientific Name: *Taxus baccata*
Family: Yew
Form: Very old trees grow up to 66 ft (20 m) high, but most remain much shorter. The shape varies; often they have an irregular crown and short, gnarled stem, so that the

branches appear close to the ground. Over 75 cultivars are available.

Needles: Soft, ¾–1½ in (2–4 cm) long; flat, linear, with a suddenly tapering sharp point; upper side dark green, shining, with prominent middle ridge, underside yellow- or gray-green and grooved (without lines). On upward-bending branches the needles grow spirally around the twig, on side twigs they are arranged in two rows (parted).

Flowers: The yew is dioecious!

Fruits: Nutlike seeds, which are surrounded by a red, cup-shaped "pseudo berry." This feature is reflected in the Latin name *baccata*, which means "provided with berries."

Bark: Red-brown to purple, thin and peeling skin-like.

European Larch

Stately tree with cone-shaped crown. The habitats of the European larch are the Alps and the Carpathians, where it is especially magnificent and grows right up to the tree line. It can live to be 600 years old. Planted in many places as an ornamental tree, the European larch is also economically important as a forest tree. The unusually hard wood is used for lumber for building and manufacturing. In fall the leaves turn a shining yellow and then drop.

Scientific Name: *Larix decidua*
Family: Pine
Form: Straight trunk with upright tip, up to 115 ft (35 m) tall; the lower half often free of branches. The branches are horizontal, somewhat down-pointing.
Twigs: Yellowish the first year.
Needles: On the long twigs they grow singly; on the short ones in bunches. Soft; ⅖–1 in (10–30 mm) long; light green (never bluish!), gray-greenish on undersides.
Flowers: The female flowers are little crimson-red cones.
Cones: Light brown; egg-shaped; up to 1½ in (4 cm) long. Cone scales not curled over.
Bark: Thick; gray-brown, often flecked with red-brown; deeply furrowed; peeling in scales.

(top) The needles are blue-green on both sides and situated on cushion-like short stems in bunches, as if stuck together. (center) A branch with one-year-old and several-year-old cones. (bottom) The trunk is reddish-gray-violet; the branches extend more or less horizontally.

Similar Species: Japanese larch (*Larix kaempferi*). In habit similar to *L. decidua*. The Japanese larch has become naturalized in a broad area of Europe, not only in parks, but also in the forests. In locations with enough moisture in the air and the ground it is superior to the European larch. The uses of the wood are the same as those of *L. decidua*.

Form: Branches not pendent, the upper ones turning upward. In old trees the crown is broad.

Twigs: In first year reddish-brown-orange, often frosted.

Needles: Blue-green on both sides, ¾–1⅖ in (20–35 mm) long; soft; undersides two gray lines, otherwise like *L. decidua*.

Cones: Brown, almost spherical, up to 1½ in (4 cm) long; the cone scales are curled backward at the edges.

Atlas Cedar

Cedars have certain similarities to larches: for one thing in growth habit, and for another in the arrangement of the needles, which grow in thick bunches on short stems. Like the larches the cedars are also mountain trees. Their habitats are the mountain areas of the Mediterranean region and Asia: Lebanon, Turkey, Cypress, Afghanistan, and the Himalayas. The Atlas cedar, which comes from the North African Atlas Mountains and forms thick forests there at elevations of 3280 ft (1000 m), has been planted as an ornamental tree in mild climates of southern Europe since the middle of the 19th century. It also thrives in protected locations in central Europe. The form "Glauca," with its intense blue needles, has shown itself to be particularly robust and grows in places that are unsuitable for other cedar species or forms. To identify the cedars (there are three main species besides the several hybrid forms), the needles are primarily considered, because the growth of the tree is often so individual that recognition on the basis of the overall form—especially with old trees—is very difficult.

(top) The needles grow in bunches on the so-called short twig, which forms only a small bump. The needles are stiff and sharp and somewhat bluish-green. (center) The cone pictured is that of the previous year. (bottom) When young the bark is smooth; this picture shows an older tree.

Scientific Name: *Cedrus atlantica*
Family: Pine
Form: Up to 131 ft (40 m) tall;

juvenile trees loosely cone-shaped with upright top growth, later irregular. Older trees often have several trunks; branches irregular and growing steeply upward; the form "Glauca" is distinguished by strikingly extended, spar-like branches.

Twigs: Thickly haired, yellowish, side-twigs not dependent.

Needles: ½ to almost 1 in (15–25 mm) long; bunched on short stems; growing separately on long twigs; stiff and sharp; bluish-green (in "Glauca" steel-blue).

Cones: 2–2¾ in (5–7 cm) long; barrel-shaped, with flat or indented tip; in first year light green, in second light brown; erect; after ripening the cones fall from the tree.

Bark: Gray and smooth when young, later somewhat grooved.

Cedar of Lebanon

When fully mature, this tree, with its broadly outspread table-like branches, is usually broader than it is tall. It comes from Lebanon and the Taurus Mountains in Asia Minor and grows there at elevations of up to 6562 ft (2000 m). Old specimens in Lebanon have been estimated to be 2000 to 3000 years old. In the first half of the 17th century the cedar of Lebanon was brought to Europe and used as an ornamental tree. Since the tree is not winter-hardy everywhere, it mainly thrives in Mediterranean areas, in western France, and southern England. Probably *Cedrus libani* is not at all the famous tree of the ancients, for its wood is soft and not so long-lasting as they had described it. Because of its good smell, the true cedar wood was at that time used for incense; or it was made into boxes for precious items. The shavings and the resin were used for embalming the dead. The word *cedar* comes from the Greek *kedros*, which originally referred to a type of juniper.

(top) The bunched needles on the short twig are typical of all cedars. In the cedar of Lebanon they are stiff and sharp. (center) The barrel-shaped cones, flattened at the end, are light green the first year, later dark brown. Cedar cones do not hang down but stand erect on the branch. (bottom) The trunk has long grooves in the bark.

Scientific Name: *Cedrus libani*
Family: Pine
Form: Up to 66 ft (20 m) tall, cone-shaped when young, later flat-crowned and spread into umbrella shape. Trunk multiple with age, branches ex-

tended far sideways and growing in flat, tablet-like planes.
Twigs: Slightly hairy.
Needles: ½–1 in (15–30 cm)
long; bunched on short stem;
stiff, sharp; usually dark green.
Cones: 3–4½ in (8–12 cm)
long; flattened or indented at
end; first light green, later dark
brown with coating of resin.
Bark: Finely grooved, dark
gray.

Deodar Cedar

(top) Typical features of the deodar cedar are drooping branches with their soft needles, which are longer than those of any other cedar. (bottom) The cones stand erect on the branches and become reddish-brown when mature.

The pendulous branches distinguish the deodar cedar from all the other cedar varieties. This is especially noticeable in young trees; with age they more resemble other cedars in habit: the Atlas or the cedar of Lebanon. The tree comes from Afghanistan and the Himalayas, where it grows at elevations of up to 6562 ft (2000 m). It was considered holy by the Hindus (the variety name *deodara* comes from *devadara*, which means something like "tree of god.") Because of its decorative appearance it was imported to Europe at the beginning of the 19th century and used in parks and gardens, especially in Mediterranean regions. In central Europe this tree is seen only occasionally, growing where climatic conditions are particularly favorable. It is extraordinarily difficult to tell the various types of cedars apart. The growth forms of older trees are often so similar to each other, or individual trees so idiosyncratic and departing from the "norm," that even an expert cannot be certain. Since the needles can also differ, even within the same variety, this clue to identification is often very unreliable as well. "Normally," the deodar cedar is recognizable by the weeping branches and the relatively long, soft needles.

Scientific Name: *Cedrus deodara*
Family: Pine
Form: Up to 66 ft (20 m) tall. In its native habitat up to 164 ft (50 m), cone-shaped when young, with pendent branch tips, later a broad crown. Trunk with horizontally extended branches; the limbs are spread out in table-like layers.
Twigs: The young shoots are thickly haired; the tips of the side shoots droop.
Needles: 1–2 in (30–50 mm) long; bunched on a short stem; pointed but soft; bluish-green.
Cones: 3–4½ in (8–12 cm) long; barrel-shaped, with blunt, non-sloping tip; at first frosted bluish, later reddish-brown. There are around 10 cultivars, blue hybrids among them.
Bark: Finely fissured; dark gray-brown.

(top) The sharp needles, often somewhat twisted, grow from a common leaf sheath in pairs. (center) The cones are relatively small and, as do most conifer cones, spread open when ripening and during dry spells. (bottom) The bark is gray-brown, later reddish-brown on upper part of trunk.

The distribution area of the Scotch pine reaches from the Pyrenees across central Europe to the Caucasus, central Siberia to the Amur region, and north all the way to Lapland. Its adaptability—it grows as well in gravely sandy soil as in peaty soil—is the reason for this worldwide expansion. The Scotch pine can live to be 300 years old; because of its strong root system with a deep-reaching taproot, it is especially wind-resistant. The wood has important economic value as lumber for construction of all kinds as well as for fiberboard, paper production, and, not least, as firewood. Turpentine and rosin are produced from the resin of the Scotch pine (and other conifers). The tree is widely planted as a forest tree, especially where the soil's poor quality rules out the use of other forest trees. But the Scotch pine is often also planted in parks and gardens because of its ornamental shape, which is reminiscent of the southern umbrella pine. Furthermore, there are several horticultural forms that differ from the species type in size, growth form, and needle color.

Scientific Name: *Pinus sylvestris*
Family: Pine
Form: Up to 131 ft (40 m) tall, at first cone-shaped, later

broadly spreading, almost umbrella-shaped. Trunk often bent when freestanding, long and straight when in forests, with lower branches shed.

Twigs: Greenish, later gray-brown; smooth.

Needles: In pairs; 1½–3 in (4–8 cm) long; stiff and sharp; thickly growing; usually twisted and half-round in cross section. The flat side is usually gray-green, the curved side dark green.

Cones: Only 1–2¾ in (3–7 cm) long; stemmed; pendent; gray-brown, matt; scales flat or slightly curved with stubby umbo; the cones drop after one year.

Mugo Pine

(top) A branch with brown-yellow (male) flowers and purple female flowers, from which the cones later develop. (center) Two cones with spread cone scales. (bottom) The trunk of the mountain pine is bent in an arch; the bark does not peel.

The Mugo pine has many forms. Depending on its geographical location, soil conditions, and elevation, it is either a low-growing bush (scrub at the tree line) or a small, often multiple-trunked tree. It can also form a straight trunk with an overall cone shape. There are three subspecies that are classified according to such differences: (1) the dwarf pine (*Pinus mugo* var. *pumilio*); (2) the crooked shrub pine (*P. mugo* var. *mughus*); and (3) the swamp pine (*P. mugo* var. *rotundata*). A fourth subspecies, the mountain pine (*P. uncinata*) is also described as a separate species. It is a tree form and grows in southern Germany or along the edges of high moorland. The habitats of all these Mugo pines are the Alps, the Swiss Jura, the Black Forest, the Vosges, the Bohemian forest, the Fichtel Mountains, the Riesengebirge, Erzgebirge, the Carpathians, and the Balkans; each region has often developed its own special form. Mugo pines grow in limestone as well as in primary rock up to an elevation of 8202 ft (2500 m). The often impenetrable clumps of mountain pine trees or scrub in the high mountains hinder erosion on the stone slopes and protect against avalanches. Besides occurring in the mountains, this pine is

frequently planted in rock gardens. There are several cultivars.

Scientific Name: *Pinus mugo*
Family: Pine
Form: Low-lying or upright, as *P. uncinata* growing to tree height of 66 ft (20 m). The trunk is bent in a curve or is perpendicularly straight.
Twigs: Bare, not frosted.
Needles: In pairs from one leaf sheath; 1–3 in (3–8 cm) long; stiff, with blunt tips; green on both sides (in *P. unciata* slightly blue-green); densely grouped.
Cones: Widely varying: ¾–2¾ in (2–7 cm) long; round, egg-, or cone-shaped; with or without stem; green at first, later brown; often with sharp cross-ridge and thorn, or else hook-shaped umbo.
Bark: Dark gray, rough, non-peeling.

Austrian Pine

(top) The long needles, which sometimes grow in pairs from a single leaf sheath, are situated on upward-bending branches. (center) Ripe cones spread their scales in dry spells (as do almost all cones). (bottom) The bark of the trunk is deeply furrowed and black-brown to red-violet.

As a result of its widespread geographic distribution, the Austrian pine has developed numerous subspecies that are difficult to differentiate from one another. The development of such subspecies is promoted by the existence of widely isolated growth zones. Thus, the subspecies *Pinus nigra ssp. nigra* grows in Austria and in the western Balkans; subspecies *laricio* in Corsica, southern Italy, and Sicily; subspecies *pallasiana* in Asia Minor, in the Crimea, and in the Caucasus; subspecies *salzmannii* in the region of the Pyrenees; and *dalmatica* on the coast and islands of northwestern Yugoslavia. The most representative is the subspecies described here, ssp. *nigra*, the Austrian pine, also known as *Pinus nigra* var. *austriaca*. The Latin name, which means black pine, refers to the totally dark impression produced by the tree's dark green needles and the blackish bark. It is very hardy and adaptable and is, for example, suited for the forestation of dry, steep slopes since it prefers alkaline soil. The wood is rich in resin and is therefore unaffected by humidity. The Austrian pine is the most important source of resin (turpentine) and can live for as long as 600 years.

Scientific Name: *Pinus nigra*
Family: Pine
Form: 66–131 ft (20–40 m) tall, oval shape, as thick at the top as at the bottom, later umbrella-shaped. Short trunk; branches upward-sloping and dense.
Twigs: Smooth, bare; at first greenish, later yellow-brown or gray-brown.
Needles: In pairs from one leaf sheath; 3–6 in (8–15 cm) long; stiff, with sharp, often yellowish points, dark green.

Cones: Up to 3 in (8 cm) long; projecting horizontally; stemless; barrel-shaped; scales with sharp ridges and a small thorn.
Bark: Black-brown to red-violet; coarsely furrowed with thick ridges; scaly.

Umbrella Pine

An unusually ornamental and picturesque pine tree that, with its umbrella-shaped crown, is one of the characteristic growth forms on the coasts of the Mediterranian and the Atlantic (Portugal). Indeed, these regions are the native habitat of the Umbrella pine. They grow singly in gardens and parks and also in forests, but always in the vicinity of the coast, as they need a mild, damp climate. For this reason this umbrella pine also flourishes in Ireland and southern England. In the United States it can only be grown from Virginia south. The wood is poorer in resin than the other pines and is used for construction and for making furniture. The seeds—"pine nuts"—are edible raw and roasted. Representations of the rounded, many-scaled stone pinecones are known to have been artistic motifs as far back as the Assyrians, Greeks, and Romans, often as ornaments for fountains or crowning buildings. In earliest Christianity the picture of the pinecone was used as the symbol for the well of life.

(top) Umbrella pines have long, pointed needles, which occur in pairs and, rarely, also in threes. (center) The rounded cones are very regularly formed; at first greenish, they later become brown. (bottom) The bark scales off in large vertical chips; underneath, the trunk is red-brown.

Scientific Name: *Pinus pinea*
Family: Pine
Form: Up to 82 ft (25 m) high; in youth with roundish crown, in age spread out in umbrella shape. Trunk often quite short

and even at lower levels divided into a few strong limbs, which then extend into outspread horizontal branches.
Twigs: Bare; gray-green at first, then brown.
Needles: In pairs from a single leaf-sheath; up to 8 in (20 cm) long; dark gray-green; sharply pointed; young trees have thinner, somewhat bluish needles.
Cones: Fat and roundish; up to 5½ in (14 cm) long and 4 in (12 cm) wide; brown and somewhat glossy. The scales are roundly curved, often with a sharp cross-ridge or several ridges, which extend radially from the umbo and divide the scale into six sections. The umbo is flat but may also protrude and is bent in something of a hook shape.
Bark: Reddish-gray and grooved lengthwise; later with large vertical plates that often peel off, revealing a reddish underlayer.

Maritime Pine

An important tree of the western Mediterranean area and the southern European Atlantic coast: Italy, southern France, Spain, Portugal. In these coastal regions the Maritime pine is found in similar locations to the Aleppo pine and, like it, is planted in forests for soil retention. The Maritime pine grows also on sandy soil, dunes, and rocky ground. It is relatively easy to recognize by its long, stiff needles and its very large, numerous pinecones, which often appear to be in grotesque disproportion to the size of the tree. The Maritime pine holds the record among native pines of Europe for length of needles and size of cones. The wood is not very durable and is used for masts, railroad ties, posts, and for the production of paper. Like many other conifers, its resin is also used for production of turpentine, especially in western France, where it is grown for this purpose. In the United States it can be grown only from Virginia south.

Scientific Name: *Pinus pinaster*

Family: Pine

Form: Up to 131 ft (40 m) tall, mostly lower, however; crown loose, broad; branches in whorls, extending horizontally; the lower part of the trunk is very nearly free of branches,

(top) Branches with male flowers. The needles are stiff and very long. (center) Since the cones can remain on the tree all year before they fall, the cluster pine is covered with generations of cones. (bottom) The bark of the trunk is furrowed into rectangular plates.

even when freestanding.

Twigs: Bare, pale to reddish-brown, at the rear end nearly without needles and over the rest unevenly patterned with needle pillows.

Needles: In pairs from one leaf sheath; up to 6 in (15 cm) long; thick, stiff, and very sharp; half-round in cross-section; dark green.

Cones: Up to 8½ in (22 cm) long; oval- to cone-shaped; light brown, glossy; the umbo of the cone scale usually projects in a hook-shaped point; the cones remain on the tree for many years, often making the tree overfull.

Bark: At first light gray, later red-brown; thick and with deep cracks, which divide the bark into square plates.

Aleppo Pine/Jerusalem Pine

The Aleppo pine is found in the coastal region of the Mediterranean and the mountains of the surrounding areas. Its growth zone extends from Spain to Asia Minor (the name comes from the city of Aleppo in Syria). It is one of those pines that are always easy to recognize: The "cloud-shaped" crown and the whitish, light branches are the characteristic hallmarks of the Aleppo pine; in addition, on closer examination there are the cones with their typical coloration. The tree is very undemanding and hardy and tolerates the drying coastal winds well. On the slopes of hills and mountains the pine performs the important function of preventing erosion. Unfortunately, both smaller and larger stands are repeatedly the victims of forest fires during the dry seasons. Turpentine is obtained from the resin of the Aleppo pine, and the wood is used for furniture and boat building. As far back as the time of the ancient Greeks, the wood of the Aleppo pine was used for building ships.

(top) The needles of the Aleppo pine are thin and soft—cones from many years hang from the branches of the tree. (center). Young cones are green, older ones red-brown with a white umbo on the scale. (bottom) This trunk shows the residue of the silver-gray bark that covers the young trunk and branches.

Scientific Name: Pinus halepensis
Family: Pine
Form: Up to 49 ft (15 m) high in youth narrow, later broad and roundly arched. Trunk often gnarled and bent, branches twisted. Crown of old trees

irregular, rounded, or spread out umbrella-like.

Twigs: Thin; greenish-brown or orange.

Needles: Pairs from one leaf sheath; up to 4 in (10 cm) long; very thin, soft, and flexible; light green; in bunches at the end of twig.

Cones: Up to 4 in (10 cm) long; on short, thick, arching stems; pointed oval; red-brown, glossy, with light gray umbo on the cone scales; often in threes; they remain on the tree for many years, so that an abundance of cones indicates age.

Bark: At first silver-gray, then reddish brown; in age deeply furrowed; bark of the limbs and branches light gray, almost white

Swiss Stone Pine/Russian Cedar

The Swiss stone pine is at home in Europe and in Asia. In Europe it is found in the Alps and the Carpathians, where it occurs mostly at altitudes between 3937 and 6562 ft (1200 and 2000 m), singly or in small groups, in Asia in the Altai Mountains and in large dense stands between the Urals and Lake Baikal. It prefers locations in primitive rock, grows slowly, and can live to be 600 years old. The yellowish, close-grained, tough wood is very much prized for wood working and for the production of furniture and sounding boards for musical instruments. The word *cembra* in the scientific name is the name of a place, Cembra, in the valley of the same name north of Trent. The Swiss stone pine is seldom planted except in gardens and parks. Thus, as time passes the natural stands are shrinking—because of the desirable wood—to only a few specimens that remain from the once extensive forests.

Scientific Name: *Pinus cembra*
Family: Pine
Form: Up to 82 ft (25 m) tall; in older trees the crown is usually multiple-topped and broad (candelabrum). The trunk is gnarled and thick in proportion to the height. When tree is freestanding, the branches

(top) The Swiss stone pine always has five needles arising from one common leaf sheath. (center) Shortly after flowering the cones appear bluish-violet, but they already have the characteristic shape. (bottom) The branches slant up from the trunk at a steep angle.

grow to the ground.
Twigs: Thick, covered with white to rust-yellow fuzz, which later darkens.
Needles: Up to five in one leaf sheath; 2–3 in (5–8 cm) long; triangular in cross-section; dark green outside, blue-white inside; primarily on the ends of branches in thick bunches.
Cones: 2–3 in (6–8 cm) long; grow only on very old trees! They are light cinnamon brown, the scales thick and wide.
Bark: At first gray-green and smooth, later dark brown and furrowed.

(top) The white pine belongs to the five-leaved pines; the needles are very thin and soft and have blue-white lines on the underside; they point in all directions and do not arch down (as in the Himalayan white pine). (bottom) The cones are very large, slightly curved, and full of sap spots.

The eastern white pine with its soft, long, brightly glistening needles and the thick, height-seeking growth is an especially decorative tree and easy to differentiate from the other pines. Its native habitat is eastern North America in the region of the Great Lakes, and the New England states up into Canada. The tree was discovered during the exploration of Maine in the early 17th century, and it became an important export product for the Massachusetts Bay Colony because the straight, long trunk was used for the masts of sailing ships. The white pine was also planted in Europe. Various favorable characteristics like fast growth, straight trunk, and soft, scarcely shrinking wood (suitable for cabinetwork and carving) make it a leading tree in many parts of Europe. Also, it is prized as a park tree. Unfortunately, it is very susceptible to blister rust. Healthy trees can live to be more than 200 years old. There are also horticultural forms. *Strobus*, from the Greek *strobos*, means "whirlwind, twisted," and refers to the spiral arrangement of the cone scales.

Scientific Name: *Pinus strobus*
Family: Pine
Form: Up to 164 ft (50 m) tall, at the beginning cone-shaped,

later broader. Straight trunk; branches on old trees very long, extending horizontally in regular whorls.

Twigs: Thin; greenish; finely haired; later brown.

Needles: Up to five from one leaf sheath; 2–4 in (5–10 cm) long; very thin; soft; straight; upper sides light green, blue-white lines on both sides underneath.

Cones: Very large, 4–8 in (10–20 cm) long; sometimes somewhat curved (banana shaped); green at first, then violet and in the second year, brown; cone scales large and leathery, usually smeared with whitish dried resin.

Bark: Smooth at first, shining, gray-green, later dark brown and with long furrows.

Himalayan Pine

(top) The needles are very thin and soft; unlike the white pine, they hang down rather "limply." The Himalayan white pine is one of the five-leaved pines. (bottom) The very large sap-smeared cones look quite similar to those of the white pine.

The soft, drooping needles of the Himalayan pine are its hall mark. Otherwise it can be confused with a young white pine, with which it has in common the large cones and its "five-leavedness." This especially decorative tree, which comes from the Himalayan regions and with other conifers forms dense forests there at heights between 6572 and 13,123 feet (2000 and 4000 m). It is found in European parks and gardens, not only in the mild climate of the Mediterranean regions, but also in central Europe. It was introduced in Europe around 1820. The scien tific name honors the Danish-English botanist Nathaniel Wallich, who, at the beginning of the 19th century, was active primarily in India. The Himalayan pine can live to be 150 years old. Attempts to grow it in forests are under-way.

Scientific Name: *Pinus wallichiana*
Family: Pine
Form: Height up to 98 ft (30 m); in youth fully cone-shaped, later a loose crown. In older trees the lower part of the trunk is branchless.
Twigs: Bare; light green, later brownish-yellow.
Needles: Up to five from one leaf sheath; 4–7 in (10–18 cm) long; very thin; on the end of

shoot pointing forward, otherwise drooping; greenish-white;
triangular in cross-section.
Cones: 6–12 in (15–30 cm)
long; slightly curving; covered
with resin; at first light purple-
red, later light brown. Cone
scales long, wrinkled, somewhat thickened.
Bark: At first smooth, dark
gray, later fissured, peeling in
thin scales.
Note: Besides confusion
between *P. wallichiana* and the
white pine *(Pinus strobus)*, it is
also possible to confuse it and

the Macedonian pine *(Pinus
peuce)*. This tree is native in
Yugoslavia, Albania, and
Bulgaria. The needles are
shorter: 4 in (10 cm) long, stiff,
and do not droop. The cones
are only 3–5 in (8–12 cm)
long; otherwise, however, they
are very similar to the Himalayan and the Eastern white pine.
The cone scales are ridged.

Italian Cypress

(top) It is easy to see that the "branchlets" are not spread out flat (as with the arborvitae) but extend in all directions; scale leaves are close-lying. (bottom) The cones of the cypress are green at first, then dark brown and glossy; in the center (on the umbo) the cone scales have a small, pointed spine.

This tree originally came from Persia, Asia Minor, and Greece but is today widely distributed all over the Mediterranean region. The "wild Mediterranean cypress" (Cupressus horizontalis) which has branches that extend sideways, producing its disheveled shape, is considered a variety or form of C sempervirens Italian cypress. The Italian cypress can grow to be more than 2000 years old (sempervirens means "ever living"). As far back as the second century B.C., the tree was considered holy in Iran because of its flame shape. The Phoenicians made ships from the wood and the Romans and Greeks made temple doors, memorial tablet and coffins from it. It played a role in death cults as a tree of grief and even today is planted in cemeteries as well as in parks and gardens. The wood is prized for fine cabinetmaking because it is hard and dense.

Scientific Name: Cupressus sempervirens
Family: Cypress
Form: Very narrow, almost columnar in shape; trunk up to 66 ft (20 m) high and strongly branching, bare at lower part.
Twigs: The branchlets are no flat but rectangular in cross section and are oriented in all directions.

Needles, Scale Leaves:
Juvenile plants have needles,
adult plants only scale leaves,
close-lying, with a long furrow
on the back; almost without
scent, even when rubbed.

Cones: Lumpy-oval; up to 1½
in (4 cm) long; pentagonal
cone scales, which bear a tiny
sharp spine; at first greenish,
then dark brown, finally gray-
brown.

Bark: Thin, gray-brown, fissured.

Similar Species: C. macro-
carpa (Monterey cypress),
C. glabra (smooth-barked
Arizona cypress), C. torulosa
(Himalayan cypress), C.
lusitanica (Portuguese or
Mexican cypress or
Cedar-of-Goa) grow in regions
with mild climates, have somewhat broader growth and
rounded tree tops.

Lawson Cypress/Port Orford Cedar

Lawson cypresses can easily be confused with thujas or Italian cypresses, and even with some juniper species. Many have the slender, conical form. For the layperson the cones or fruits may be the simplest means of differentiation. In the Lawson cypresses they are ball-shaped and small; in the *Thuja* species also small but cup-shaped; in the Italian cypresses lumpy-egg-shaped and larger (½–1½ in (1–4 cm), while the juniper species in this category have fleshy "pseudo berries." The Lawson cypress was introduced to Europe in the middle of the 19th century from Oregon in the northwestern United States and has since spread widely, especially in gardens and parks. The wood is yellowish, firm, enduring, fragrant, and prized as commercial timber.

There is a very large number of ornamental forms (about 130), which are very difficult to identify. They differ from the type described here in color, branch form, and in total habit.

(top) When the branchlets are examined in a cross light, the oil glands that are located in the center of the scale leaves can be seen. (center) The juvenile (this year's) cones are bluish and only later become brown. (bottom) The branches extend horizontally from the trunk, which is vertically fissured.

Scientific Name:
Chamaecyparis lawsoniana
Family: Cypress
Form: Narrow cone-shaped; up to 98 ft (30 m) high; when freestanding, branches all the way to the ground. Trunk frequently forked; short branches extending horizontally.

Twigs: Green at first, later reddish-brown. Flat branchlets covered with scale leaves and branching only in one plane are situated on the twigs. These scale leaves have a transparent oil gland in the center and are dark green on the upper side and paler on the underside. The canted scale leaves sit with the point up.

Cones: Roundish; numerous; about ⅓ in. (8 mm) thick; green at first and frosted with bluish-white, later purplish-brown; the cone scales have small ridges.

Bark: At first smooth and dark brownish-green; later fissured in long, vertical scales and reddish.

(top) A branch with young cones. Unlike cypresses, the branch spreads in one plane only. (center) The older conelets are brown and spread away from each other; they often appear so numerous that they almost obscure the green of some of areas of the tree. (bottom) The trunk is reddish-brown, scaly.

There are six *Thuja* species, all of which originate in North America and the Orient. The *occidentalis*, the American arborvitae, comes from the Western hemisphere but it has been naturalized in Europe for a long time (since 1550) and has been planted in parks and gardens. Today, there exist a large number of cultivated forms, which vary as to the color, branch form, and the habit of the arborvitae. This useful tree allows itself to be pruned into any form, making it popular for use in evergreen hedges. Its Latin name, meaning "tree of life," derives from the medical use of the "oil of Thuja" that is obtained from its branches.

Scientific Name: *Thuja occidentalis*
Family: Cypress
Form: Thin cone-shaped with upright crown branches; height up to 66 ft (20 m). Often multiple-trunked, branched to the ground.
Twigs: Branching in one plane, the branchlets are compressed flat.
Scale Leaves: Closely arranged, like roof tiles. Upper sides dark green, dull-glossy, undersides pale green, dull; when rubbed, resiny-fruity smelling. The scales on the broad side have clearly visible (translucent) oil glands.
Cones: About ½ in (1 cm) in

size; oval; at first greenish, in second year brown and cup-shaped, spreading away from each other.

Bark: Gray-brown; tears off in small strips.

Similar Species: The giant arborvitae (*Thuja plicata*), also known as the giant cedar or western red cedar, is native to North America and is not only grown in parks and gardens but, because of its wood, is also an important forest tree. It can live to be 800 years old and is very similar in habit to *Th. occidentalis*. The outstanding differences are: The giant arborvitae grows up to 131 ft (40 m) high and the tip of the adult tree is broader and the trunk is widened at the base. The bark is dark reddish-brown. Scale leaves are bright green on the upper side and glossy; the undersides are whitish, often without oil glands, and have a strong, fruity smell.

Comparison of Cone Shapes

1. Cedar of Lebanon
   Cedrus libani
2. Atlas cedar
   Cedrus atlantica
3. Norway spruce
   Picea abies
4. Douglas fir
   Pseudotsuga menziesii
5. Italian cypress
   Cupressus sempervirens
6. American arborvitae
   Thuja occidentalis
7. Giant sequoia
   Sequoiadendron giganteum
8. Giant arborvitae
   Thuja plicata
9. Oriental spruce
   Picea orientalis

10. European larch
    Larix decidua
11. Japanese larch
    Larix kaempferi
12. Smooth-barked Arizona
    cypress
    Cupressus glabra
13. Nootka cypress
    *Chamaecyparis
    nootkatensis*
14. Colorado blue spruce
    Picea pungens
15. Serbian spruce
    Picea omorika
16. Engelmann spruce
    Picea engelmannii
17. Lawson cypress
    Chamaecyparis lawsoniana

1. Mugo pine/*Pinus mugo*
2. Macedonian pine
   Pinus peuce
   normally longer
3. White pine
   Pinus strobus
4. Himalayan pine
   Pinus wallichiana
5. Austrian pine
   Pinus nigra
6. Scotch pine/*Pinus sylvestris*
7. Aleppo pine
   Pinus halepensis
8. Maritime pine
   Pinus pinaster
9. Western hemlock
   Tsuga heterophylla
10. Canada hemlock
    Tsuga canadensis
11. Swiss stone pine
    Pinus cembra
12. English yew/ *Taxus baccata*
13. Umbrella pine
    Pinus pinea

How to Use This Book

The most commonly cultivated conifers of Europe are presented in *Barron's Coniferous Trees*. They are also cultivated in the United States. They are divided into three groups, each identified by a color code. Color photographs show the general appearance and all the details of the tree that are important for identification. Brief, easy-to-understand descriptive text gives a picture of the exact appearance; a short introductory text provides useful information about the origin and location, as well as special details about the tree under discussion. Pages 60–61 illustrate the cones, which also may provide a definitive clue for recognition of a conifer. Identification is therefore made easy even for the beginning botanist.

Meaning of the Color Code

The colored coding marks beside the tree portraits are an additional identification aid.

 Conifers with a *single needle on a twig*.

 Conifers with *needles bunched* on a short twig; these bunches consist of 2, 3, 5, or more needles.

Conifers with *scale-shaped leaves*.

Explanation of the Descriptive Text

The commonly used English name of the tree appears over the small pictures on the lefthand page; in some cases one or two other common names also appear. The caption under the small pictures gives the botanical information illustrated in the photographs. After the introductory text follow the **Scientific Name** and, under **Family,** the English name of the plant family. The appearance is described in detail under the headings **Form, Twigs, Needles, Cones,** and **Bark.** The heading **Similar Species** points out similar tree species, which are also briefly described there.

The Author:

Georg Zauner, born in 1920, painter and graphic artist, later author and producer of numerous popular-scientific films.

Coniferous Trees Index

Abies
  alba, 2–3
  concolor, 8–9
  nordmanniana, 4–5
  procera, 6–7
Aleppo Pine, 46–47
American Arborvitae,
  58–59
Atlas Cedar, 30–31
Austrian Pine, 40–41

Cedar of Lebanon,
  32–33
Cedrus
  atlantica, 30–31
  deodara, 34–35
  libani, 32–33
Chamaecyparis
  lawsoniana, 56–57
Colorado Blue Spruce,
  20–21
Common Juniper,
  24–25
Cupressus
  sempervirens, 54–55

Deodar Cedar, 34–35
Douglas Fir, 10–11

Eastern White Pine,
  50–51
English Yew, 26–27
European Larch, 28–29

Giant Redwood, 22–23
Giant Sequoia, 22–23

Hemlock, 12–13
Himalayan Pine, 52–53

Italian Cypress, 54–55

Jerusalem Pine, 46–47
Juniperus communis,
  24–25

Larix decidua, 28–29
Lawson Cypress, 56–57

Maritime Pine, 44–45
Mugo Pine, 38–39

Noble Fir, 6–7
Nordmann's Fir, 4–5
Norway Spruce, 14–15

Oriental Spruce, 16–17

Picea
  abies, 14–15
  omorika, 18–19
  orientalis, 16–17
  pungens, 20–21
Pinus
  cembra, 48–49
  halepensis, 46–47
  mugo, 38–39
  nigra, 40–41
  pinaster, 44–45
  pinea, 42–43
  strobus, 50–51
  sylvestris, 36–37
  wallichiana, 52–53
Port Orford Cedar, 56–
  57
Pseudotsuga menziesii,
  10–11

Russian Cedar, 48–49

Scotch (Scots) Pine,
  36–37
Sequoiadendron
  giganteum, 22–23
Serbian Spruce, 18–19
Silver Fir, 2–3
Swiss Stone Pine,
  48–49

Taxus baccata, 26–27
Thuja occidentalis,
  58–59
Tsuga canadensis,
  12–13

Umbrella Pine, 42–43

White Cedar, 58–59
White Fir, 8–9
White Pine, 50–51

All inquiries should be addressed to:
Barron's Educational Series, Inc.
250 Wireless Boulevard
Hauppauge, New York 11788

Library of Congress Catalog Card No. 90-20154

International Standard Book No. 0-8120-4451-7

Library of Congress Cataloging-in-Publication Data

Zauner, Georg, 1920–
  [Nadelbäume. English]
  Coniferous Trees / by Georg Zauner; translated by Elizabeth D. Crawford.
    p. cm — (Mini fact finders)
  Translation of: Nadelbäume.
  ISBN 0-8120-4451-7
  1. Conifers—Europe—Identification. 2. Conifers—Europe-Pictorial works. 3. Conifers—Iden-
tification. 4. Conifers—Pictorial works. I. Title. II. Series.
QK494.Z3813 1991
585'.2'094—dc20
                                                                                    90-2015
                                                                                    CI

PRINTED IN HONG KONG
1234 4900 987654321

The photographs: (c = center, t = top, b = bottom, r = right, l = left)
Pforr: 14 c, 24 t, 24 b, 25, 26 t, 28 c, 38 t, 49, 50 t, 56 c, back cover;
Riedmiller: 2 c, 3, 4 cl, 4 cr, 5, 6 t, 6 c, 7, 8 c, 10 c, 12 c, 16 c, 17, 18 c, 20 c, 22 t, 22 c, 28 t, 30 c,
30 b, 31, 32 c, 32 b, 33, 35, 36 t, 38 c, 40 c, 40 b, 42 c, 44 t, 44 b, 46 t, 48 c, 52 b, 53, 54 t, 56 t,
58 t, front cover;
Scherz: 23;
Zauner: 2 t, 2 b, 4 t, 4 b, 6 b, 8 t, 9, 10 t, 10 b, 11, 12 t, 12 b, 13, 14 t, 14 b, 15, 16 t, 16 b, 18 t,
18 b, 19, 20 t, 20 b, 22 b, 26 c, 26 b, 27, 28 b, 29, 30 t, 32 t, 34 t, 34 c, 36 c, 36 b, 37, 38 b, 39,
40 t, 41, 42 t, 42 b, 43, 44 c, 45, 46 c, 47, 48 t, 48 b, 51, 52 t, 55, 56 b, 57, 58 c, 58 b, 59